ANIMALS THAT LIVE ON THE FARM / ANIMALES QUE VIVEN EN LA GRANJA

Sheep/
Las ovejas

JoAnn Early Macken

Reading consultant/Consultora de lectura:
Susan Nations, M.Ed.,
author/literacy coach/consultant

WEEKLY WR READER®
EARLY LEARNING LIBRARY

Please visit our web site at: www.earlyliteracy.cc
For a free color catalog describing Weekly Reader® Early Learning Library's list
of high-quality books, call 1-877-445-5824 (USA) or 1-800-387-3178 (Canada).
Weekly Reader® Early Learning Library's fax: (414) 336-0164.

Library of Congress Cataloging-in-Publication Data

Macken, JoAnn Early, 1953-
    (Sheep. Spanish & English)
    Sheep = Las ovejas / JoAnn Early Macken.
        p. cm. — (Animals that live on the farm = Animales que viven en la granja)
    Includes bibliographical references and index.
    ISBN 0-8368-4290-1 (lib. bdg.)
    ISBN 0-8368-4297-9 (softcover)
    1. Sheep—Juvenile literature. I. Title: Ovejas. II. Title.
    SF375.2.M3312   2004
    636.3—dc22   2004054982

This edition first published in 2005 by
Weekly Reader® Early Learning Library
330 West Olive Street, Suite 100
Milwaukee, WI 53212 USA

Picture research: Diane Laska-Swanke
Art direction: Tammy West
Cover design and page layout: Kami Strunsee
Translators: Colleen Coffey and Consuelo Carrillo

Photo credits: Cover, pp. 13, 15, 21 Gregg Andersen; pp. 5, 11 © Daniel Johnson;
p. 7 © Norvia Behling; p. 9 © Alan & Sandy Carey; p. 17 © James P. Rowan;
p. 19 © Adams/Hansen Photography

Printed in the United States of America

2 3 4 5 6 7 8 9 10 09 08 07 06

Note to Educators and Parents

Reading is such an exciting adventure for young children! They are beginning to integrate their oral language skills with written language. To encourage children along the path to early literacy, books must be colorful, engaging, and interesting; they should invite the young reader to explore both the print and the pictures.

Animals That Live on the Farm is a new series designed to help children read about the behavior and life cycles of farm animals. Each book describes a different type of animal and explains why and how it is raised.

Each book is specially designed to support the young reader in the reading process. The familiar topics are appealing to young children and invite them to read — and re-read — again and again. The full-color photographs and enhanced text further support the student during the reading process.

In addition to serving as wonderful picture books in schools, libraries, homes, and other places where children learn to love reading, these books are specifically intended to be read within an instructional guided reading group. This small group setting allows beginning readers to work with a fluent adult model as they make meaning from the text. After children develop fluency with the text and content, the book can be read independently. Children and adults alike will find these books supportive, engaging, and fun!

Una nota a los educadores y a los padres

¡La lectura es una emocionante aventura para los niños! En esta etapa están comenzando a integrar su manejo del lenguaje oral con el lenguaje escrito. Para fomentar la lectura desde una temprana edad, los libros deben ser vistosos, atractivos e interesantes; deben invitar al joven lector a explorar tanto el texto como las ilustraciones.

Animales que viven en la granja es una nueva serie pensada para ayudar a los niños a conocer la conducta y los ciclos de vida de los animales de la granja. Cada libro describe un tipo diferente de animal y explica por qué y cómo se cria.

Cada libro ha sido especialmente diseñado para facilitar el proceso de lectura. La familiaridad con los temas tratados atrae la atención de los niños y los invita a leer — y releer — una y otra vez. Las fotografías a todo color y el tipo de letra facilitan aún más al estudiante el proceso de lectura.

Además de servir como fantásticos libros ilustrados en la escuela, la biblioteca, el hogar y otros lugares donde los niños aprenden a amar la lectura, estos libros han sido concebidos específicamente para ser leídos en grupos de instrucción guiada. Este contexto de grupos pequeños permite que los niños que se inician en la lectura trabajen con un adulto cuya fluidez les sirve de modelo para comprender el texto. Una vez que se han familiarizado con el texto y el contenido, los niños pueden leer los libros por su cuenta. ¡Tanto niños como adultos encontrarán que estos libros son útiles, entretenidos y divertidos!

— Susan Nations, M.Ed., author, literacy coach,
and consultant in literacy development

A **lamb** is a baby sheep.
Lambs run, jump, and play.

- - - - - - - -

El **cordero** es una oveja
recién nacida. Los corderos
corren, saltan y juegan.

Lambs drink milk from their mothers. Later, they can live on grass.

- - - - - - - -

Los corderos se alimentan con la leche de la madre. Más tarde se alimentan con hierba.

A **ewe** is a female sheep. A ewe knows its lamb by the smell.

— — — — — — —

La **oveja** es la hembra del ovejo. La oveja conoce a su cordero por el olor.

In summer, sheep can stay outside. A group of sheep is called a **flock**.

- - - - - - -

En el verano, las ovejas se quedan a la intemperie. Un grupo de ovejas se llama **rebaño**.

In winter, sheep may stay in a shed or a barn. The farmer feeds them hay or grain.

— — — — — — — —

En el invierno, las ovejas se quedan en el cobertizo o granero. El granjero les da de comida, heno o granos.

Not all sheep are white.
Some sheep are black,
brown, or gray.

- - - - - - -

No todas las ovejas son
blancas. Algunas son
negras, marrones o grises.

Sheep have thick wool coats. A sheep's coat is called its **fleece**. It never stops growing.

- - - - - - - -

Las ovejas tienen capas gruesas de lana. Esta capa gruesa de lana se llama **vellón**. Nunca deja de crecer.

Some farmers raise sheep for meat. Some farmers raise sheep for their wool. These sheep are having their fleece **sheared**, or cut.

－－－－－－－－

Algunos granjeros crían las ovejas para carne. Otros las crían para lana. Estas ovejas están siendo **esquiladas**.

Some farmers raise sheep for their milk. Have you ever seen sheep on a farm?

— — — — — — —

Algunos granjeros crían ovejas para leche. ¿Alguna vez has visto ovejas en una granja?

Glossary/Glosario

grain — seeds or fruit from grass plants
grano — semillas o frutas de plantas

hay — grass that is cut and dried for food
heno — hierba que se corta y se seca para comida

sheared — cut
esquilar — cortar la lana

shed — a small building used for shelter or storage
corbertizo — pequeña construcción que se usa como refugio o almacenaje

For More Information/Más información

Books/Libros

From Sheep to Sweater. Start to Finish (series).
   Robin Nelson (Lerner)

Hooray for Sheep Farming! Bobbie Kalman
   (Crabtree)

Sheep. Farm Animals (series). Rachael Bell
   (Heinemann)

Sheep on the Farm. On the Farm (series).
   Mari C. Schuh (Capstone)

Web Sites/Páginas Web

Spring Lambs
*www.cyberspaceag.com/visitafarm/photoessays/s
pringlambs/default.htm*
Pictures of sheep and lambs

Index/Índice

About the Author/Información sobre la autora

JoAnn Early Macken is the author of two rhyming picture books, *Sing-Along Song* and *Cats on Judy*, and four other series of nonfiction books for beginning readers. Her poems have appeared in several children's magazines. A graduate of the M.F.A. in Writing for Children and Young Adults program at Vermont College, she lives in Wisconsin with her husband and their two sons. Visit her Web site at www.joannmacken.com.

JoAnn Early Macken es autora de dos libros infantiles ilustrados en verso, *Sing-Along Song* y *Cats on Judy*, y también de cuatro series de libros de corte realista dirigidos a los lectores principiantes. Sus poemas han sido publicados en varias revistas para niños. Graduada del M.F.A. en Redacción para niños y adultos jóvenes del Vermont College, vive en Wisconsin con su esposo y sus dos hijos. Visita su página Web. www.joannmacken.com.